MW01345852

Living
Artfully

Living Artfully

Inspired by Tradition

for roger—
enjoy!
♡ shannon

Shannon Carter

photography by Ryan Kurtz

ORANGE *frazer* PRESS
Wilmington, Ohio

ISBN 978-1939710-284

Published for the author by:
Orange Frazer Press
P.O. Box 214
Wilmington, OH 45177
Telephone: 937.382.3196 for price and shipping information.
Website: www.orangefrazer.com
Book and cover design: Alyson Rua and Orange Frazer Press

Printed in China
Second Printing
Library of Congress Control Number: 2015941033

Proceeds from the sale of *Living Artfully, Inspired by Tradition* will benefit the Taft Museum of Art, Cincinnati, Ohio.

To my loving husband, Lee;

to our wonderful children, Gunner and Cody,

and their spouses, Anne and Seth;

to our darling grandchildren, Liza, Cooper, and Alice;

and to our parents and grandparents

who taught us to appreciate and respect tradition.

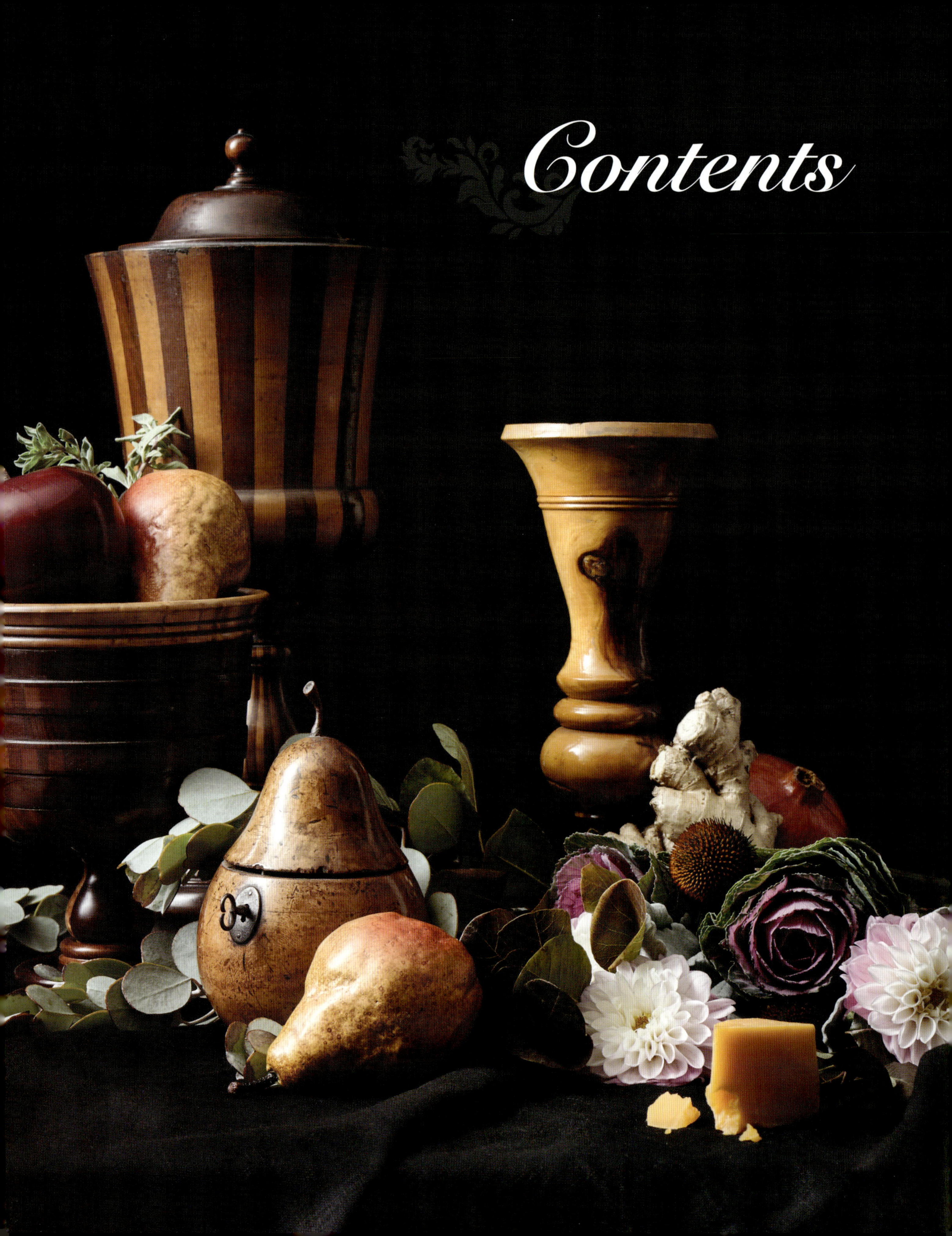

Contents

viii Introduction

1

12 *Collections*
14 Tiny Treasures
26 Pretty Porcelains
34 Beautiful Brass & Books
42 Splendid Surfaces
50 Everyday Ceramics
58 Country Charm

2

64 *Tradition*
66 Enjoying Heirlooms

3

74 *Recipes*
76 Appetizers
98 Soups
120 Salads
142 Sides
164 Entrées
186 Desserts

4

208 *Entertaining*
210 Having Fun

220 *Thank You*
223 *Recipe Index*

Introduction

"Someday you will appreciate these, dear,"

"Someday you will appreciate these, dear," was my mother's comment on my birthdays in the 1950s and 1960s as I was growing up. Each year I received as a present from my godmother a monogrammed silver butter plate. It certainly was not the doll or book I had hoped to unwrap twelve consecutive times. In fact, admittedly, some years I never bothered to open Aunt Pat's annual gift.

Not until I was in my thirties did I begin to appreciate those dozen silver butter plates. Early on, I used them to help fill book shelves in my single's apartment. After I was married, I happened to set the table for a dinner party at home using the butter plates and our guests raved about them! That was a defining evening for me when I took stock of those silver presents as well as the treasured heirlooms that my husband, Lee, had brought into our marriage.

Setting a table with decorative flowers, linens, dishes, stemware, and cutlery is similar to building a store display. Details and presentation are everything, as I learned in my first retailing career, and that has become a lifelong creative outlet and passion. Cooking and styling good food is another fascination that has become an enjoyable hobby to share with family and friends over the years.

Hence this book, *Living Artfully, Inspired by Tradition*, is a personal story of appreciating beauty and grace. It is a gift to my children, grandchildren, friends, and anyone who shares my interest in collections and the enjoyment of using heirlooms at home.

The recipes in the third section are family favorites handed down from my grandmother and mother as well as from friends and long ago cooking classes. Some have been updated and improved upon by those who helped me prepare and present the food for this book. Most of the photographs are the way I serve food for our family or when entertaining. Using inherited serving pieces or antique accessories from our collections and including a dash of whimsy are priorities for presentation.

The final section of the book is about "having fun," an attitude we have about entertaining and enjoying our friends. I have highlighted a few special invitations and fun food presentations for parties and events hosted over the years.

By sharing stories, recipes, and ideas, I hope to inspire my children and grandchildren to love living artfully, because "someday you will appreciate these, dears."

Living Artfully

Collections

How fortunate I have been to have had three separate careers all of which contributed to my appreciation of the fun of discovery.

My first career, at age 22 and fresh out of college in the early seventies, was merchandising and marketing Pappagallo shoes and clothes. What fun it was to decorate a Hyde Park Victorian home with period furniture to display and sell the colorful boutique line of shoes and matching accessories. Frequent buying trips to New York were the chase to find the cutest and latest fashions that filled the preppy bill at the time. Each season marked a new beginning of color and style trends that were fresh and exciting.

My second career, as a sales associate, was merchandising shipments of beautiful English antiques and smalls. The chase this time was annual buying trips across the pond with my mother's dear friend, Mary March, who owned a charming shop in a 19th century, historically registered house in Montgomery, Ohio. The fun was buying for customers who had specific requests, finding beautiful treasures, and learning about the history of English furniture and accessories. I grew to truly value the craftsmanship and artistry of fine pieces and objects handcrafted in England centuries ago. This experience also enhanced my respect for tradition, my appreciation for heirlooms, and the enjoyment of living with antiques.

My third career, as one of the founders of a non-profit teacher's free store, was merchandising school supplies and distributing them at no cost to educators. The chase for this inventory was to collect the community's surplus, outdated or slightly damaged products, often destined to a landfill. In a spacious warehouse we operated a retail store without a cash register. Teachers would "shop" four afternoons a week for supplies, using them creatively in their classrooms for underserved students.

For me, the chase has always been the fun of discovering, buying, or collecting that special piece, whether for others or for my family. Designing attractive spaces and creating appealing displays for customers at work or tablescapes and surprises for guests at home have been a life-long passion.

The following pages highlight my collection of miniatures that have provided years of enjoyment for myself and my family.

The chase has always been the fun of discovering, buying, or collecting that special piece…

Tiny Treasures

Collecting Miniatures

I was fascinated by the intricate details of its design, its weight, and its extraordinary craftsmanship . . .

My journey of collecting miniatures began in 1986 when my husband, Lee, gave me as a present a miniature silver tea set, made entirely by hand in the 1930s by William B. Meyers.

I was fascinated by the intricate details of its design, its weight, and its extraordinary craftsmanship on a scale of one inch to twelve.

William Meyers, a noted American silversmith, (1887–1956) was the sole owner, at age 26, of his New Jersey silver firm making distinctive pieces of holloware. When his competitors began to copy his original designs, he started making reproductions of famous Georgian silver pieces found in museums and in private collections and sold them to better silver dealers and fine department stores. The trade loved these copies and begged for more.

When the Depression gripped the country in 1929, Meyers was forced to reduce his payroll, sell his machinery, and resort to making copies by hand. He wanted to have a personal collection of his fine silver reproductions, but because of space constraints, he decided to make miniature scaled copies. In his spare time, he painstakingly incorporated every detail and decorative element and even made copies that functioned exactly like the full scale originals.

Pleased with his results and wanting an artistic opinion, Meyers showed some samples to one of his customers, Emma Haig, a New York interior decorator.

She was smitten with what she saw and promptly ordered as many pieces as he could produce.

Americans had not yet become fascinated with this silver hobby until Emma Haig sold them to her high end clients. Meyers' miniature business led to a new and exciting career. Collectors clamored for these Georgian reproductions, and Meyers hired more than a dozen craftsmen to fill the avalanche of labor intensive orders.

By 1937, Meyers began identifying his trademark with an "M," "Sterling," and "Handmade" imprint on every piece possible. It is estimated that he made about 400 different miniature silver objects, mostly serving pieces. Shirley Temple and Eleanor Roosevelt were known to be among the many collectors of Meyers' miniatures.

The dealer from New Hampshire at the Cincinnati Antiques Festival who sold Lee the tea set later became a dear friend.

Children's Banks

The Dutch excelled in making fine miniature furniture in the late 17th century...

Acquiring the Meyers' silver tea set was just the beginning of my lifelong journey collecting miniature pieces. Its small scale and intricate details not only appealed to my fun childhood memories of playing dolls, but also to my appreciation of the craftsmen who had the patience and skill to make these unique works of art.

The second miniature I obtained was a small mahogany chest, 5½ inches tall, with ivory knobs. It was actually a child's bank and my first purchase from Mary March English Imports.

On her inaugural trip abroad, Mary had bought the miniature chest/bank with a specific friend in mind, but when her client declined the piece, I spoke up for it. I was fascinated not only by the charm of its quality and details, but also by the fact that most miniature furniture was made as playthings for doll houses, as children's toys, or for parents' sheer enjoyment. The Dutch excelled in making fine miniature furniture in the late 17th century, and the craze for anything small moved to England a century later and eventually to America.

Miniature chests of drawers were particularly popular to hold trinkets, ribbons, gloves, etc., and in this case, they functioned as a child's bank.

The pages that follow illustrate a variety of English banks, desks, and other miniature furniture that we have had the pleasure of collecting over the years.

A miniature George II style mahogany kneehole desk rests on a small Georgian walnut kneehole desk, circa 1730.

Two pairs of Lyre back silver candlesticks, one standard size and the other miniature by William Meyers.

A Tale of Two Desks

...two rare companion pieces are together after almost 300 years. If only those desks could talk!

The two fine walnut miniature desks, circa 1720, are believed to be apprentice pieces either made by separate cabinet makers working side by side in the same carpenter shop or possibly one craftsman who improved his skill and design over time.

Both desks were coincidentally acquired from the same dealer in England. The first purchase occurred on an early buying trip with Mary March. Eleven years later, I received an overseas telephone call from a gentleman with a distinguished English accent. He asked me, "Are you Mrs. Carter, the miniature lady from Ohio?" After I replied, "Yes," he said, "I have the most extraordinary bureau that I think you might like." After his detailed description of the desk, I asked him to please send me a picture for consideration. The photograph arrived and I could not believe my eyes! The miniature desk was almost identical to the one I had bought from him on my trip with Mary.

The dealer believes that the apprentice(s) made the miniature desks either to serve as his personal masterpieces or to advance his apprenticeship for better employment. The reason he does not think that they were salesman's samples was that he had never seen, in his forty years in the trade, a standard size desk with an interior design of "checkered ground in sycamore and bog oak." To him, this unique interior was simply a mark of quality craftsmanship.

Early salesman's samples, some of them in their original carrying cases, were made as practical smaller versions of their full size counterparts. A cabinet maker could visit his customers on their country properties and discuss the requirements for their furniture orders. By the end of the 18th century, many cabinet makers like Chippendale and Sheraton had produced pattern books or catalogues which were much easier for travelling salesmen to transport around the countryside.

Andrew Jenkins was the dealer in England, whom I visited several times later, and he continues to be as excited as I am to know that two rare companion pieces are together after almost 300 years. If only those desks could talk!

The following pages illustrate the similarities and differences between the two miniature desks.

Similarities
10" wide,
11" high,
5" deep
Interior cupboard with
checkerboard detail and
center mirror
Rich walnut patina
Rectangular
hinged slant
front top
Drawers with stringing detail
and original brass pulls
Rectangular top drawer over two
short and three graduated drawers

Differences
Rich leather instead of informal felt
More pronounced curved center arch
Stringing detail inlay on bureau top
More pronounced shaped bracket feet
More formal keyhole escutcheons

Pretty Porcelains

Famille Rose soup tureen, stand, dinner plates, platter, and bowl.

Eighteenth century Chinese export porcelain pieces from a marriage service. Two American market pieces, a spoon tray, and a covered cream jug, both with American eagles.

The homeowner was met at the front door by her housekeeper who said, "I have some good news and bad news. The bad news is that I broke your china ship bowl, but the good news is that it was really old."

ELECTI
NON
FRANCI

New Hall, Worcester, and Chinese export porcelains.

A large Japanese Kutani plate and Sacred Bird and Flower pattern plates.

Beautiful Brass & Books

A tin tea caddy in the form of bound books rests on a mahogany book carrier.

Nineteenth century brass banks were made in a variety of shapes and sizes.

A collection of decorative brass wall pockets used to store matches.

OBRAS
III
LORNA DOONE
BLACKMORE
WAVERLEY NOVELS 41.
THE HIGHLAND WIDOW.

Splendid Surfaces

A George III mahogany tea caddy in the form of a bow front chest of drawers with a harewood shell medallion, boxwood stringing, and shaped bracket feet.

A George I inlaid burl walnut miniature chest on stand and a Queen Anne style walnut chest on chest.

A George II miniature walnut desk, a George I walnut chest of drawers, and an 18th century fruitwood tea caddy in the shape of a pear.

A collection of English boxes, tea caddies, and tortoise ware.

Everyday Ceramics

Country Charm

A collection of children's chairs and wooden stools.

A collection of country banks.

Vintage country kitchen tools, one of which was my mother's doll spatula.

Tradition

2

Webster's dictionary defines an heirloom as "a valued family possession handed on from generation to generation." It may be a fine piece of furniture, an exquisite silver container, or a beloved jewelry item. No matter what the object, the craftsmen who made these items were exceptional artists of their day, creating beauty that we all appreciate years later.

The generations who have preceded us enjoyed furnishings, accessories, serving pieces, and objects for every detail in life especially at the dining table. There were lavish silver candelabra and stately champagne coolers, beautiful porcelain urns for fruit, elaborately etched trays, punch bowls and soup tureens, specific silver forks for sardines and slotted spoons for nuts and candy, special receptacles for personal butlers to collect cigarette ends, and even engraved silver handled scoops to brush away crumbs from linen tablecloths. The Victorians of the late nineteenth century enjoyed the pomp of entertaining during the high point of silver's popularity.

For the silver items that escaped being melted down in the 1980s, many may well be tarnishing in locked closets or remain idle in pantries or drawers. For me, these items are pieces of history and traditions that need to be revived, respected, and enjoyed.

The following section features several heirlooms that have been re-purposed for today's use. They maintain their sentimental value while being relevant in our 21st century active lives. The photographs present ideas for entertaining and suggestions for everyday use. In the recipe section of this book, there are dozens of ideas for food to be served in silver, porcelain or wood dishes of yesteryear, including the use of heirloom cutlery. Mixing and matching antiques with contemporary pieces adds a surprise element to presentations, delights guests, and makes occasions more memorable.

It is fun to view heirlooms as treasures and to give them new life. It is a matter of "re-framing" our minds to appreciate valued family possessions and to live life more artfully.

It is fun to view heirlooms as treasures
and to give them new life...

Enjoying Heirlooms

Offices do not have to be so office like! When organizing supplies in a desk drawer, it is more fun to use a silver vegetable serving dish than a plastic divided tray. • Victorian silver toast racks and brass hand clips are a great way to keep notes and invitations. • Vintage ink wells and magnifying glasses still serve a purpose in today's world. • A brass bound wine cooler holds decorative pillows in a library while a peat bucket is the perfect container for current magazines.

A favorite shell collection finds a home in a silver fruit basket. • Brass wall pockets double as flower containers. • Brass monteiths, originally used to chill wine glasses, house potpourri while a seldom used silver asparagus serving piece holds a music collection of CDs and tapes.

Cocktail snacks and condiments served in vintage wood or silver heirloom pieces take on a new relevance. • An engraved treasured family trophy holds lemons at a makeshift bar.

Add fun touches to a buffet table setting with whimsically displayed silverware or cutlery and napkins presented in antique wood carriers.

Guest towels in a lavatory are displayed in a mahogany tea caddy. • Cotton balls and swabs are placed in a biscuit barrel and an earthenware container while guest soaps occupy a French bowl. • Various pills find homes in vintage brass, treen and silver boxes, the latter of which housed cigarettes years ago.

Sewing supplies are conveniently organized in miniature chests of drawers. • A vintage mink stole is reused in a coat designed by Koos of New York. • Silver candy containers are used as a festive centerpiece for an afternoon tea party.

shop for Pappagallo
holiday recipes
Shop for Pappagallo
JUDGE BLACKMORE'S FAVORITE RECIPES
Shop for Pappagallo
Bulk Rate
U.S. Postage
Shop for Pappagallo
The POPPY'S PAPPAGALLO
FESTIVAL FARE
The 1986 Cincinnati
the shop for Pappagallo
favorite recipes
favorite family recipes
compiled especially for cody and gunner

Recipes

3

The chase for keeper recipes has been, again, the fun of discovering special treasures from the past and savoring those traditions today. Handwritten recipes, especially ones on stained cards from my mother's and grandmother's recipe boxes always give me pause.

Years ago I started collecting favorite family recipes and organizing them into booklets. My first recipe booklet was a hand drawn keepsake giveaway for a political campaign used instead of matchbook covers that were common at the time.

After this gimmick distribution proved successful, I drew seasonal Pappagallo catalogues and weekly newspaper advertisements to promote the brand and our products. I also drew recipe booklets for annual shoe and clothing sales. The four by six inch mailers, fit for recipe boxes of the era, were almost as popular as our inventory, and to this day, many former customers still have their copies and rave about the timeless recipes.

My third attempt at marketing with recipes was the Cincinnati Antiques Festival that I chaired in 1986 when Martha Stewart was our featured guest speaker. I received permission to reprint one of her recipes in a booklet, again hand drawn, that we used to promote the show and her lecture. What an easy and inexpensive tool to gain audiences and to deliver a great message about the important work at Convalescent Hospital for Children, the Festival's beneficiary.

In 1999, when I was at Crayons to Computers, a teacher's free store, we compiled the recipes of all of our dedicated volunteers. We produced a printed, spiral bound booklet containing a few hundred of our volunteers' favorite dishes. We enjoyed the publication internally and shared it with the organization's product and financial donors.

Over the course of the last ten years I have handwritten several booklets of family recipes for our children's households and for our use. They are a quick reference and fun to have on hand.

The sixty plus recipes that follow are all family favorites passed down or shared over the decades by relatives and friends. Several are easy or old fashioned, and many are just comfort food. While today we try to nourish ourselves in healthier ways, we still enjoy foods with decadent ingredients and serve them with pride and joy to our favorite guests.

. . .to this day, many former customers still have their copies and rave about the timeless recipes.

Appetizers

Parmesan Tuilles

Baby Beets Topped with Boursin Cheese

Black Olive Curry Canapés

Radicchio Cups with Bleu Cheese

Mini Cocktail Quiches

Seafood Cocktail Spread

Oyster Crackers with Seasoning

Spicy Tortilla Wraps

Parmesan Puffs

Watercress Sandwiches

Parmesan Tuilles

Packed with Parmesan flavor, these lacey treats are easy and delicious. Transferring them quickly from the oven to a wire rack is important.

Makes 12 crisps

1 cup Parmesan cheese
1 tsp. flour
½ tsp. black pepper

Preheat oven to 450 degrees F.

Combine cheese, flour and pepper in a bowl. Mix thoroughly.

Place 2 tablespoon mounds of cheese on a non-stick cookie sheet. Press down with fingers arranging the mounds into strips 2 inches wide.

Place cookie sheet in oven for 5 minutes or until cheese has melted and is bubbly brown. Cheese should not be gooey, but one solid crisp.

Remove from oven and immediately lift cheese off cookie sheet with a heat resistant spatula.

Cool on a wire rack.

Serve on a pretty platter at room temperature.

Baby Beets
topped with Boursin cheese

Using canned beets, which are small and consistent in size for a one bite appetizer, makes this recipe very easy. It is fun to also serve them in a silver silent butler or on a treasured heirloom tray.

Makes about 22

2 15 oz. cans small beets
1 5.2 oz. package of Boursin (garlic and herbs) cheese
parsley, freshly chopped

Drain beets and cut off bottom to stand upright.

Scoop out top portion of beet and spoon in a dollop of Boursin cheese.

Garnish with freshly chopped parsley.

Chill and serve.

Black Olive
Curry Canapés

This recipe is clipped from a 1979 Gourmet Magazine. It doubles as an appetizer and a warm open faced sandwich. Still yummy after all of these years!

Makes 48

1½ cups black olives, minced
½ cup mayonnaise
2 tbsp. onion, minced
¼ tsp. curry powder
1 cup sharp cheddar cheese, grated
6 English muffins, halved
½ cup finely chopped green onion (garnish)

Preheat oven to broil.

In a bowl, combine black olives, mayonnaise, onion, and curry powder. Stir in cheddar cheese and mix thoroughly.

Lightly toast English muffin halves, top down. Remove from oven.

Spread mixture onto halves untoasted side up.

Place under broiler 3 inches from the top and cook 3–4 minutes or until bubbly.

Quarter each muffin and transfer to a serving plate.

Garnish with finely chopped green onion after baking.

Radicchio Cups

with Bleu cheese

These are colorful, unique and delicious canapés. Embellished with additional greens such as arugula, frisee, or curly endive, the recipe becomes a great salad.

Makes 16

1 cup crumbled bleu cheese
¼ cup black walnut pieces, toasted
1 tbsp. mayonnaise
¼ cup parsley, chopped
2 heads radicchio lettuce
salt and pepper to taste

Mix together cheese, nuts, mayonnaise, and parsley in a bowl.

Season to taste with salt and pepper.

Divide mixture and spoon onto radicchio leaves, trimmed to canapé size.

Chill and serve.

Mini Cocktail Quiches

Men, especially, like this hearty hors d'oeuvre. They are better made in the morning, chilled and reheated just before serving.

Makes 24

1 tube of 8 small refrigerated flaky buttermilk biscuits
½ cup mayonnaise
3 pieces fried bacon, chopped (½ cup)
1 medium tomato, seeded and chopped (½ cup)
1 tbsp. minced onion
1½ cups Swiss cheese, shredded
2 tsp. fresh basil, chopped

Preheat oven to 375 degrees F.

Divide each biscuit into 3 layers or 24 pieces.

Place each biscuit slice into non-stick mini-muffin cups. Set aside.

Combine mayonnaise, bacon, tomato, onion, cheese, and basil in a bowl. Mix thoroughly.

Divide the mixture evenly among the 24 mini-muffin cups pressed with dough.

Bake until golden brown, about 15–20 minutes. Remove from cups and cool on wire rack.

Can be easily made ahead of time, chilled and reheated.

Seafood Cocktail Spread

Your choice of seafood can be layered between this easy, herbed cream cheese mixture and cocktail sauce topped with chopped parsley. It can also be served in individual cups.

Serves 12

2 8 oz. packages of cream cheese
¼ cup mayonnaise
1 tbsp. fresh lemon juice
1 tbsp. minced onion
1 tbsp. Worcestershire sauce
1 tsp. Tabasco sauce
1 dash garlic salt
½ lb. of fresh, cooked shrimp, crabmeat or lobster
1 bottle of chili or cocktail sauce
2 tbsp. fresh parsley, chopped

Mix together well the first 7 ingredients.

Spread on bottom of ceramic pie dish.

Layer fresh seafood onto mixture.

Spread sauce over seafood and garnish with chopped parsley.

Best made a day before.

May need to drain excess liquid.

Serve with crackers.

roger

Oyster Crackers
with Seasoning

These crackers are a family favorite and a perfect teacher or hostess gift during the holidays. Children and now grandchildren delight in pouring all of the ingredients into a brown paper bag and shaking it with gusto. It presents well in a cellophane bag tied with festive ribbons.

Serves 25

1 14 oz. box oyster crackers
⅔ cup safflower oil
1 package ranch dressing mix
1 tsp. dill weed

Combine all ingredients in a large bowl.

Transfer to a brown paper bag. Shake bag to mix thoroughly.

Best made in advance. Store at room temperature.

Spicy Tortilla Wraps

Make these easy wraps the day before serving. Slices can be one or two bites. The salsa for dipping is key.

Makes up to 6 dozen

6 12 inch flour tortillas
2 8 oz. packages cream cheese, softened
1 4 oz. can chopped green chilies
1 4 oz. can chopped black olives
2 tbsp. salsa
2 tbsp. minced dried onions
1 tbsp. chopped fresh coriander (half to garnish)
pinch of chili powder

Mix together all ingredients.

Spread onto tortilla shells. Roll tightly and refrigerate.

Slice into one-inch or larger diagonal pieces and garnish with chopped coriander.

Serve with fresh salsa.

VERITAS
10
NESTED
BISCUIT

Parmesan Puffs

Cheese puffs are everyone's favorite and they have been popular for decades. I cherish the recipe card in my grandmother's handwriting where she suggests that adding minced onion is optional.

Makes 6 dozen

1 cup mayonnaise
1 cup Parmesan cheese, grated
¼ cup minced onion (optional)
1 loaf white bread
1 tsp. paprika

Preheat oven to 200 degrees F.

Mix mayonnaise, Parmesan cheese, and onion in a bowl.

Cut bread rounds from 1½ inch round cookie cutter.

Bake 5 minutes until bread top is dry. Turn bread rounds upside down and continue baking until other side is also "dry" (not toasted).

Spoon dollop of cheese mixture onto each round. Sprinkle with paprika.

Can prepare up to this point and chill.

Broil until bubbly.

Serve hot.

Watercress Sandwiches

These classic tea sandwiches are always a hit with guests. The trick is to gently roll the soft white bread so that it flattens but does not become too soggy when spreading the cream cheese mixture.

Makes 36

1 bunch watercress
8 oz. cream cheese
2 tbsp. horseradish sauce
1 loaf of soft white bread
Kosher salt

Remove base stems from watercress leaving tender leaves.

Save a handful of watercress sprigs for each sandwich.

Blend together watercress, cream cheese, and horseradish sauce. Salt to taste.

Cut crusts off of bread. With a rolling pin, gently roll each piece of bread thinly.

Spread mixture over bread inserting watercress sprig on each end.

Roll sandwich and cut in half.

Chill and serve.

Soups

Curried Cream Cheese Consommé

Cold Tomato Soup

French Onion Soup

Simply Enhanced Soups

Butternut Squash and Ginger Soup

Garden Green Soup

Iced Borscht

Vichysoisse

Gazpacho

Minted Pea Soup

Curried Cream Cheese

Consommé

This recipe always makes a big hit whether served as an appetizer in a shot glass or as a first course at a dinner party. Preparing it in a plastic old fashioned glass makes it also a perfect summer treat for an alfresco terrace meal.

Serves 4 as first course
Serves 8 as appetizer

1 8 oz. package of cream cheese
1 tsp. curry powder
1 tsp. fresh lemon juice
1 10½ oz. can beef consommé, divided in half
stuffed green olives, sliced (garnish)

Mix cold cream cheese, curry powder, lemon juice, and half of the consommé in a blender. Process until smooth.

Pour into 4 shot glasses or demitasse cups.

Chill three hours or until firm.

Dividing equally, pour remaining consommé over mixture in cups.

Chill until firm.

Garnish with olive slices.

Cold Tomato Soup

This recipe is so easy and flavorful. Passed down through the family decades ago, it remains a staple for summer fare. It is best made the day before.

Serves 4

1 can undiluted tomato soup
1 can beef broth
8 oz. sour cream
2 tbsp. green onion, chopped
½ cucumber, peeled and seeded
1 tbsp. red wine
½ tsp. salt
1 tbsp. fresh basil leaves
4 tbsp. sour cream (garnish)
½ cucumber thinly sliced (garnish)

Mix all ingredients in a blender and chill well.

Best made the day before.

Garnish with a dollop of sour cream and cucumber slices.

French Onion Soup

This recipe is attributed to Chef Jim Gregory, who in the late 1960s, conducted cooking classes for my mother and her friends. Today, many of his recipes are still used and enjoyed.

Serves 6

- 6 large yellow onions, thinly sliced
- 1 large white sweet onion, thinly sliced
- 3 tbsp. butter
- 3 tbsp. olive oil
- 1 tbsp. sugar
- 2 cans beef consommé
- 2 cans water
- ½ cup dry vermouth
- 6 slices French bread
- ¾ cups Gruyere cheese, grated
- ¾ cups Swiss cheese, grated

In a large skillet, sauté onions, butter, and olive oil over medium high heat until onions are soft and transparent.

Stir in sugar.

Add consommé and water and bring to a boil.

Add vermouth.

Let rest for one hour. Reheat when ready to serve.

Preheat oven to 350 degrees F.

For topping, toast French bread slices. Pour soup in oven proof individual crocks and place bread over soup.

Sprinkle with Gruyere and Swiss cheese.

Cook for 12–15 minutes until crust is golden, melted and bubbly hot.

Simply Enhanced

Soups

These recipes appeared in Pappagallo sales mailers in the 1970s. Doctoring up canned soups is not a novel idea. Have fun experimenting on your own.

Serves 2

Curried Chicken

To a can of cream of chicken soup, add 1 cup of light cream, 1 tsp. curry powder, ¼ cup chopped parsley, salt, and lemon pepper to taste. Simmer over low heat for 10 minutes. Salt and pepper to taste.

Cream of Mushroom

To a can of cream of mushroom soup, add 1 can of beef consommé and blend well. Simmer over low heat for 10 minutes. Add ¾ cup fresh, sliced mushrooms, sautéed in butter. Season with vermouth. Salt and pepper to taste.

Rich Tomato Bisque

To a can of tomato bisque soup, add 1 cup of milk. In a saucepan, sauté 2 tbsp. butter and 1 small onion, diced. Add 3 oz. cream cheese and stir until softened. Fold into soup. Simmer over low heat for 10 minutes. Season with a dash of dill weed.

Creamy Asparagus

To a can of cream of asparagus soup, add 1 cup of light cream and 1 cup of steamed asparagus tips. Simmer over low heat for 10 minutes. Salt and pepper to taste.

Butternut Squash
and Ginger Soup

Although this is an autumn recipe, it is delicious all year round. It can be served in a hallowed out acorn squash, miniature pumpkin, or in your favorite soup tureen. The maple syrup drizzle is a nice addition.

Serves 8–10

2½ lb. butternut squash
2 tbsp. olive oil
1 medium leek, cleaned, trimmed and cut into ½ inch pieces
1 clove garlic, minced
1 tsp. fresh ginger, minced
1 tsp. salt
¼ tsp. pepper
4 cups chicken broth
cream fraiche (garnish)
maple syrup (garnish)

Preheat oven to 350 degrees F.

Remove flesh and seeds from the squash. Place in a baking pan and bake in oven until soft, about 45 minutes.

Let cool. Remove skin and cut into small pieces.

Heat olive oil over medium heat and add leek and garlic. Sauté for 3–5 minutes.

Add ginger and squash. Cook and stir over medium heat for an additional 3–5 minutes.

Add salt, pepper, and chicken stock. Cover and bring to a boil. Reduce heat and simmer for 30 minutes or until vegetables are tender.

Pour soup into a blender or food processer to puree.

Garnish with a small dollop of cream fraiche and a drizzle of maple syrup.

Serve hot.

Garden Green Soup

Cream cheese and avocado are the thickening agents in this recipe. Using different greens can vary the flavors, so do not hesitate to use what is available from your summer garden.

Serves 4

1 shallot, peeled
2 cups torn spinach leaves
2 cups torn butter head lettuce
2 tsp. fresh lemon juice
1 avocado cut into chunks
3 tbsp. cold cream cheese
2 cups chilled chicken stock
salt and pepper to taste
fresh dill (garnish)
sour cream (garnish)

Mince shallot in food processor.

Add spinach, lettuce, and lemon juice.

Add avocado and cream cheese until smooth.

Slowly pour in chilled chicken stock.

Season to taste.

Serve chilled.

Iced Borscht

Roasting and peeling fresh beets is a labor of love, but well worth it to create this sensational chilled, summer soup.

Serves 12

12 medium beets
2 medium onions
2 carrots, finely grated
1 tbsp. unsalted butter
1 tsp. sugar
6 cups chicken broth
3 tbsp. lemon juice
2 cups sour cream
salt and pepper to taste

Preheat oven to 350 degrees.

Wash unpeeled beets.

Wrap in aluminum foil and bake for 1 hour or more until fork tender.

Cool, peel, and grate.

Sautee onions and carrots in butter.

Add beets, sugar, and broth. Simmer uncovered for 25 minutes.

Remove from heat. Cool.

Puree in food processor.

Stir in lemon juice and season with salt and pepper. Chill.

Fold sour cream into beet mixture and serve.

Save a little sour cream to decorate the soup.

Vichysoisse

This is another old fashioned favorite that never goes out of vogue. Serving it in porcelain lined silver demitasse cups repurposes a cherished heirloom.

Serves 6

2 yellow onions, sliced
2 leeks, white part only, sliced
1 bay leaf
3 tbsp. butter
2 baking potatoes, peeled and diced
4 cans chicken broth
½ tsp. Worcestershire sauce
1 dash Tabasco
1 pint whipping cream
salt and pepper

In a skillet, sauté onions and leeks in butter until soft.

Add chicken broth, bay leaf, and potatoes. Cook until potatoes are very soft.

Puree mixture in food processor.

Strain and whisk in Worcestershire sauce and Tabasco. Cool.

Add whipping cream to desired consistency and season to taste with salt and pepper.

Chill and serve.

Minted Cucumber Soup

To vichysoisse base, add 1 English cucumber and 3 sprigs of mint, finely chopped in food processor.

Gazpacho

Nothing tops this classic chilled summer favorite that is nutritious and always delectable. Add chopped, fresh herbs to vary the flavor.

Serves 8

2 stale hard rolls, soaked in cold water until soft
4 cups V-8 juice
4 large ripe tomatoes, peeled, seeded, and chopped
1 cucumber, peeled, seeded, and chopped
½ green pepper, chopped
2 scallions, chopped
3 tbsp. olive oil
1 tbsp. red wine vinegar
1 dash Worcestershire sauce and Tabasco
1 tbsp. paprika
chopped chives, parsley, basil, chervil, or tarragon (optional)
salt and pepper to taste

Squeeze moisture from bread. Place in blender or food processor. Puree on medium speed.

Add V-8 juice, tomatoes, cucumber, green pepper, scallions, olive oil, vinegar, and seasonings to taste.

Transfer to a large bowl. Chill several hours or overnight.

Serve and garnish with diced vegetables.

Minted Pea Soup

It is worth growing mint in your garden to enjoy this soup often. Serve in a bread bowl, your favorite cup or mug, or in a pretty cream soup dish.

Serves 8

1 small onion, finely chopped
2 tbsp. unsalted butter
2 lb. frozen peas
5 cups chicken broth
1 cup fresh mint leaves, packed
1 cup heavy cream
salt and pepper to taste

In a large heavy saucepan, sauté onion and butter over medium low heat.

Add peas and 3 cups of broth. Simmer, uncovered 5–7 minutes until peas are tender.

Stir in mint and remaining 2 cups of broth.

Remove pan from heat and cool slightly.

In a blender or food processor, puree soup in batches until very smooth.

Pour mixture through a sieve into a large bowl and discard solids.

Whisk in heavy cream. Add milk to thin if necessary. Salt and pepper to taste.

Chill if serving soup cold.

Reheat, but do not boil, if serving warm.

Salads

Orzo Salad with Tomatoes, Feta, and Basil

Roasted Cauliflower and Arugula Salad

Netherland Salad

Mustard Tarragon Chicken Salad

Colorado Salad

Chilled Pasta Salad with Shrimp

Asian Slaw

Watercress and Feta Salad with Curried Yogurt Dressing

Tomato Aspic

Summer Salad

Orzo Salad

with Tomatoes, Feta, and Basil

This salad is yummy as is, but it can be varied by adding black olives, cucumbers, peppers, green onions, and even roasted root vegetables.

Serves 8

- ¼ cup red wine vinegar
- 2 tbsp. fresh lemon juice
- 1 tsp. honey
- ½ cup olive oil
- 1 lb. orzo
- 6 cups chicken broth
- 2 cups cherry tomatoes, halved
- 7 oz. feta cheese cut into ½ inch cubes (about 1½ cups)
- 1 cup fresh basil, chopped
- ½ cup green onions, chopped
- ½ cup pine nuts, toasted

Whisk vinegar, lemon juice, and honey in a small bowl. Gradually whisk in olive oil. Season with salt and pepper.

Can be made 2 days ahead. Cover and chill.

Bring chicken broth to a boil in a large saucepan. Stir in orzo.

Reduce heat to medium, cover partially and boil, stirring occasionally until tender but still firm to bite. Drain.

Transfer to a large bowl, tossing frequently until cool. (Pasta will continue to cook.)

Mix tomatoes, basil, and green onions into orzo.

Add vinaigrette and season to taste.

Fold in feta cheese and pine nuts before serving.

Can be made 2 hours ahead. Let stand at room temperature.

Roasted Cauliflower
and Arugula Salad

The combination of flavors makes this contemporary salad a winner. It is great on its own or served with a grilled entrée.

Serves 4

1 head cauliflower, cut into very small florets
3 tbsp. olive oil
¼ cup Parmesan cheese, grated
1 bunch arugula
1 15 oz. can white beans
1 cup dried cranberries
½ cup almonds, toasted
½ cup safflower oil
3 tbsp. white wine vinegar
1 tbsp. fresh tarragon
salt and pepper to taste

Preheat oven to 425 degrees F.

Toss cauliflower florets with olive oil and season with salt and pepper.

Tossing occasionally, roast until almost tender 35–40 minutes.

Sprinkle with Parmesan cheese and continue roasting until tender, 10 minutes longer.

Combine arugula, beans, cranberries, almonds, and cheese in a bowl. Add cauliflower.

Make dressing by combining safflower oil, vinegar, and tarragon. Season to taste. Pour over salad before serving.

Netherland Salad

This original recipe is also called the Meurice Salad, so named after Chef Meurice at the Netherland Hilton Hotel in Cincinnati. It has remained on the hotel restaurant's menu for more than six decades and is a meal in itself.

Serves 4

Salad

1½ head Iceberg lettuce, shredded
1 cup rotisserie chicken, cut into strips
1 cup ¼ inch thick baked ham, cut into strips
½ cup Swiss cheese, cut into strips
¾ cup tomatoes, peeled, seeded, and chopped

Dressing

2 tbsp. sweet pickles, chopped
2 hardboiled eggs, chopped
6 tbsp. mayonnaise
¼ cup red wine vinegar
6 tbsp. olive oil
2 tsp. Worcestershire sauce
2 tsp. fresh chives

Optional Garnish

1 hardboiled egg, sliced
2 tomatoes, peeled and quartered

Toss lettuce with chicken, ham, Swiss cheese, and tomatoes.

Mix next 7 ingredients and pour onto lettuce mixture.

Garnish with hardboiled egg slices and tomatoes. (optional)

Mustard Tarragon
Chicken Salad

Fresh tarragon, now easily available, makes this salad truly delectable. It is more than picnic fare and could take center stage on a summer buffet.

Serves 4

1 rotisserie chicken, skinned and boned
2 cups broccoli florets, blanched
½ cup celery, chopped
1 cup cherry tomatoes, halved
1 cup mayonnaise
3 tbsp. white wine
¼ cup mustard (½ Dijon and ½ whole grain)
1 ½ tsp. fresh tarragon, chopped
salt and pepper to taste
fresh basil

Mix chicken, broccoli, celery, and tomatoes in a bowl.

Combine dressing ingredients and toss together.

Dressing absorbs best when chicken is warm.

Serve at room temperature.

Colorado Salad

The origin of this recipe was inspired by a similar salad we experienced while visiting our family in Colorado. The cornbread croutons and fresh ginger add the magic flavors to this hearty meal.

Serves 6

1 ear corn, kernels removed
1 log creamy goat cheese, crumbled
½ pint cherry tomatoes
¼ cup black olives, sliced
1 avocado, diced
1 cup corn bread croutons
1 rotisserie chicken, boned and cut into chunks
1 small head of radicchio lettuce
1 small head of butter lettuce
I small bunch of romaine hearts
½ cup fresh, chopped basil

Slice and chop lettuces.

Toss in bowl with remaining ingredients.

Serve with ¾ cup Dijon vinaigrette.

Makes ¾ cup

Dijon Vinaigrette
1 tbsp. Dijon mustard
4 tbsp. red wine vinegar
1 tsp. sugar
½ tsp. salt
½ tsp. freshly ground black pepper
½ cup light olive oil
minced parsley, optional

Measure mustard into a bowl.

Whisk vinegar, sugar, salt, pepper, and parsley.

Slowly drizzle in olive oil, whisking constantly until mixture thickens.

Best made just before serving.

Chilled Pasta Salad

with Shrimp

This colorful salad can also be made with crabmeat or lobster. The fresh dill and lemon juice give it a tangy flavor.

Serves 6

1 lb. shrimp, cooked
½ head broccoli florets
6 green onions, chopped
2 tsp. fresh dill
4 medium tomatoes, peeled, seeded, and chopped
1 tbsp. fresh lemon juice
12 oz. pasta (fusilli, rotini, or bow tie), cooked and drained
½ cup olive oil
3 tbsp. white wine vinegar
salt and pepper to taste

Combine shrimp, broccoli, green onion, dill, and tomatoes in a bowl.

Toss with lemon juice and season with salt and pepper. Let stand for 1 hour.

Add chilled cooked pasta and toss with oil and vinegar. Season, again, as necessary.

Asian Slaw

This is a tried and true recipe that is often passed over for conventional slaws or salads. The crunch from the cashews and Ramen noodles are distinctively delicious.

Serves 8

1 8 oz. bag coleslaw mix
1 8 oz. bag broccoli coleslaw mix
1 3 oz. package Oriental Ramen noodles
1 cup cashew nuts, crushed in a plastic bag with a rolling pin
½ cup canola oil
½ cup granulated sugar
¼ cup cider vinegar
2 tbsp. soy sauce season packet reserved from noodles

Preheat oven to 300 degrees F.

Toast noodles and crushed cashews 10–12 minutes on cookie sheet covered with aluminum foil. Cool.

Combine dressing ingredients in a small bowl and stir well.

In a large bowl, combine slaws, noodles, and cashews.

Toss with dressing 2–3 hours before serving.

Watercress and Feta

Salad with Curried Yogurt Dressing

This is another salad packed with flavor. The creamy curried ginger dressing provides a different texture from vinaigrettes.

Serves 4

1 bunch red leaf lettuce
1 bunch watercress, base stems removed
1 cup feta cheese chunks
2 tomatoes, quartered
½ cup black olives, sliced
1 can artichoke hearts, sliced
fresh chopped basil
grilled teriyaki chicken strips. Marinate the chicken in your favorite teriyaki overnight and grill.(optional)

Curried Yogurt Dressing

1 cup mayonnaise
1 cup plain yogurt
2 tsp. teriyaki sauce
1 tbsp. curry powder
1 tsp. fresh ginger, minced
¼ tsp. garlic, chopped
½ tsp. poppy seeds

Toss lettuce and watercress in a large bowl.

Add cheese, tomatoes, olives, artichoke hearts, chopped basil, and chicken strips.

Mix together all ingredients for salad dressing and fold into lettuce mixture.

Tomato Aspic

Most people born after 1970 do not know about tomato aspic. Lemon Jell-O is the secret ingredient to this wonderful accompaniment to chicken salad or as a colorful side to summer grilled meat or fish.

Serves 12

3 cups tomato juice
3 cups V-8 juice
12 oz. lemon Jell-O
1½ cups celery, chopped
½ cup onion, chopped
dash of lemon juice

Boil juices in a sauce pan.

Add Jell-O into hot juices. Stir well.

Add celery,onion, and lemon juice before set.

Pour into greased ring mold and chill for several hours.

Unmold and garnish as you like.

Summer Salad

Stacked or tossed, the surprising combination of herbs, fruits and vegetables makes this salad not only beautiful, but also absolutely delicious. The trick to assembling stacked ingredients is to layer them in an oiled and chilled cylindrical mold.

Serves 6

2 cups cantaloupe
3 avocados
2 cups tomatoes
2 cups strawberries, washed and trimmed
¼ cup safflower oil
2 tbsp. balsamic vinegar
2 tbsp. fresh orange juice
rind of 1 orange
salt and pepper to taste
fresh mint sprigs

Dice first four ingredients into same sized chunks.

Make dressing by combining oil and vinegar. Add orange juice, rind, salt, and pepper. Mix together thoroughly.

Toss with fruit and vegetables just before serving. Fold in chopped mint.

Drizzle dressing on top. Garnish with mint sprigs.

Sides

Creamed Spinach

Kentucky Spoon Bread

Ratatouille

Maple Ginger Roasted Vegetables

Cider Stewed Tomatoes

Popovers

Sweet Potato Mash

French Green Beans

Spiced Iced Tea

Yeast Dinner Rolls

Creamed Spinach

This is Lee's favorite of all side dishes! If you are in a hurry, combine the cooked, drained spinach with 8 ounces of cream cheese. Adding sauteed onions is a great option.

Serves 6

2 10 oz. packages of frozen chopped spinach
3 tbsp. softened butter
3 tbsp. flour
½ cup light cream
¼ tsp. nutmeg
salt to taste

Place frozen spinach in a saucepan with 1 cup of water.

Bring to a boil and cook until spinach is just thawed and still green.

Combine butter and flour in a small bowl and knead together until smooth.

Drain excess water from spinach.

Place saucepan back on low to medium heat and add butter mixture, mixing thoroughly. Cook for one minute.

Add cream and nutmeg and continue stirring while cooking 5 minutes. Salt to taste.

Fun fact:
The equal amounts of softened whole butter and flour, kneaded together in a paste, is called buerre manie. It is a quick alternative to roux which involves melting clarified butter and whisking it into flour. Both methods of butter and flour cooked briefly are thickening agents for soups and stews.

Kentucky Spoon Bread

Mary March gave this recipe to my mother in the 1960s. I grew up enjoying spoon bread and to this day, we serve it often to guests who are always pleasantly surprised. Lots of butter is the natural accompaniment.

Serves 6–8

6 cups milk
6 eggs, beaten
1½ cups sifted yellow cornmeal
2 tbsp. melted butter
2 tsp. salt
6 tsp. baking powder

Preheat oven to 350 degrees F.

Pour 4 cups of milk into a sauce pan. Add cornmeal. Stir constantly over medium heat until mixture turns to mush. Remove from stove.

Combine 2 cups of milk, well beaten eggs, melted butter, salt, and baking powder.

Pour mixture into cornmeal mush. Beat well with wire whisk.

Pour into well-greased baking dish. Bake for 45 minutes to an hour until set.

Serve hot with butter.

Ratatouille

This classic and colorful side dish embodies the best of fresh summer vegetables, and it is equally good all year round when made with a can of tomatoes.

Serves 6

1 medium eggplant, peeled, cut into 2 inch strips and salted
3 medium zucchini, cut into 2 inch strips
2 green peppers, seeded and cut into 2 inch strips
1 cup onions, thinly sliced
½ cup olive oil
2 cloves garlic, crushed
1½ tsp. salt
¼ tsp. pepper
3 medium tomatoes, peeled and quartered
½ cup chopped parsley

Preheat oven to 325 degrees F.

On a paper towel, let salted eggplant rest for 30 minutes. Drain liquid.

Sauté eggplant, zucchini, peppers, and onions separately in olive oil, garlic, salt, and pepper.

Transfer to a large casserole. Layer with tomatoes and parsley.

Bake for 1 hour. Serve hot or cold.

For variations, add croutons or mozzarella cheese on top.

Maple Ginger
Roasted Vegetables

The maple syrup and fresh ginger give these roasted vegetables a particularly rich flavor. Other options for this recipe include using fresh herbs, such as rosemary or oregano.

Serves 12

4 medium carrots (¾ pound), peeled and sliced ¼ inch thick on the bias
2 large parsnips (1 pound), peeled and sliced ¼ inch thick on the bias
1 medium head cauliflower, (2½ pounds) cut into 1-inch florets
1 small butternut squash (2 pounds), peeled, seeded, and cut into 1-inch pieces
1 pound Brussels sprouts, halved
½ cup extra virgin olive oil
¼ tsp. freshly grated nutmeg
Kosher salt, and freshly ground pepper
2 tbsp. minced fresh ginger
½ cup pure maple syrup

Preheat oven to 425 degrees F.

In a large bowl, toss the carrots, parsnips, cauliflower, squash, and Brussels sprouts with the olive oil and nutmeg. Season generously with salt and black pepper.

Spread the vegetables on 2 large rimmed baking sheets and roast for 30 minutes or until vegetables begin to brown.

Sprinkle ginger and drizzle maple syrup over vegetables and toss well.

Continue to roast for 25 minutes longer until they are tender and golden.

Scrape vegetables into a bowl and serve hot or at room temperature.

Cider Stewed Tomatoes

This recipe came from a dear friend decades ago and it remains a staple condiment surprise to guests. The trick is to spend at least two hours stirring the mixture over low to medium heat until it is ruby red. Turn up the music, have a side project, and just be patient until the tomatoes thicken.

Serves 6

2 28 oz. cans whole tomatoes
1½ cups sugar
¾ cup apple cider vinegar

Combine all ingredients in a heavy skillet and cook slowly for 2 hours or until ruby red and glazed. Stir often. Start on medium heat and then reduce to low.

Best made the day before.

Popovers

Popovers are fun to serve because they are least expected! Their presentation always draws a pleasant surprise. Investing in a proper popover pan makes this recipe almost foolproof along with never opening the oven door before they are finished baking. Butter, again, is the necessary accompaniment.

Makes 12

2 cups all-purpose flour
2 tbsp. salted butter, melted
4 large eggs, room temperature
¾ tsp. salt
2 cups whole milk

Preheat oven to 450 degrees F.

Whisk flour, butter, eggs, salt, and milk together until smooth.

Grease muffin or popover pan well.

Fill each cup halfway with batter.

Bake 30 minutes with the oven door closed at all times.

Serve immediately with butter.

Sweet Potato Mash

Sweet potatoes or cooked yams, infused with the ingredients in this recipe, have never tasted better. Beyond our Thanksgiving ritual, they are company fare with roasted pork tenderloin or other dishes.

Serves 8

3 lb. sweet potatoes (or yams)
½ cup light brown sugar, firmly packed
½ cup fresh orange juice
4 tbsp. butter, melted
2 tbsp. fresh lemon juice
2 tsp. orange zest, finely grated
¼ tsp. ground nutmeg
¼ tsp. cinnamon
½ tsp. fresh ginger, minced
¼ tsp. salt
pepper to taste

Preheat oven to 350 degrees F.

Butter a 2-quart casserole and set aside.

Pierce each sweet potato with a sharp pronged fork.

Place on baking sheet and bake in oven for an hour or longer until fork pierces sweet potatoes easily.

Cool to room temperature, peel and mash until light and fluffy.

Combine all ingredients in a large mixing bowl. Beat until smooth.

Season to taste with salt and pepper.

Transfer to casserole, spreading to the edge and roughing the surface.

Bake uncovered for 45 minutes or until tips are brown.

Drizzle with maple syrup.

French Green Beans

When most of the men in my family fill their plates on a buffet line, there is not a speck of green evident. This is a very simple recipe that makes selecting something green a no-brainer.

Serves 4

4 oz. French green beans
3 tsp. course salt
3 tbsp. butter

Prepare beans by trimming off the stem ends.

Bring water to a full boil in a large stock pot. Add beans and cook for 4 minutes.

Remove and place beans in a bowl filled with ice water. This will stop the cooking process. Drain beans once they are cooled.

Using a skillet set on medium to high heat, melt the butter halfway.

Add beans and sprinkle with salt.

Cook for another 4 minutes stirring constantly.

Serve immediately.

Spiced Iced Tea

This is another recipe my mother gleaned from the ladies at the bridge table in the 1960s. Boiling cloves is the secret. Doctored up with orange juice and zests of lemons and oranges, the tea becomes the secondary ingredient.

Makes 1 gallon

1 tbsp. cloves
3 cups sugar
2 family size tea bags
3 cups boiling water
6 cups orange juice, preferably fresh squeezed
3 lemons, squeezed
grated lemon rind of 3 lemons

In 3 quarts of water, boil cloves for 10 minutes.

Let stand up to 2 hours.

While still warm, melt sugar in clove juice.
Remove cloves.

Make tea in 3 cups of boiling water.

Add orange juice, lemon juice, and lemon rind.

Chill and serve with sliced or wedged lemons.

Yeast Dinner Rolls

Nothing beats the taste of yeast dinner rolls. Dipped in butter before baking and smothered in butter when hot, they are a decadent treat and well worth the effort.

Makes 30–36

- ½ cup boiling water
- ½ cup vegetable shortening
- ½ cup sugar
- ¾ tsp. salt
- 1 egg
- 1 package dry yeast
- ½ cup lukewarm water
- 3 cups bread flour
- 6 tbsp. unsalted butter, melted

In large bowl, pour boiling water over shortening, sugar, and salt. Mix until blended and cool.

Beat the egg slightly adding the water and shortening mixture slowly.

Combine the yeast with the lukewarm water. Allow to dissolve, stirring gently.

Combine yeast with egg mixture. Add flour, a little at a time, until well blended.

Cover with plastic wrap and refrigerate overnight.

On a floured surface, knead the dough for 2 minutes. Roll out the dough to ½ inch thick and cut with a 2 inch biscuit cutter.

Dip each roll in the melted butter. Fold in half.

Place in a buttered 10 x 14 inch pan. Let the rolls rise 1–1.5 hours to double its size.

Bake at 400 degrees for about 12 minutes until golden brown.

Break apart and serve warm with butter of course!

Entrées

Cold Steamed Salmon

Chicken & Artichokes with Mushrooms

Bavarian Beef and Noodles

Chicken Curry

Lamb Stew

Hearty Lasagna

Pork Tenderloin with Cherry Sauce

Mustard Cream Red Snapper

Chicken and Pasta Casserole

Pot Roast 1950s Style

Cold Steamed Salmon

Whether you poach or steam the salmon, it is the perfect summer dish with cucumber sauce. Served warm or cold, it always makes a hit!

Serves 4

4 8 oz. salmon fillets, boned and skin on
1 tbsp. lemon juice
salt and pepper to taste
lemon slices (garnish)
dill sprigs (garnish)

Cucumber Dill Sauce
1 cup sour cream
2 tbsp. chopped fresh dill
1 English cucumber peeled and diced
1 tbsp. lemon juice
salt and pepper to taste

Salmon

Thoroughly rinse fish in cold water and pat dry.

In a steamer with a tight fitting lid, bring 2 inches of water to a boil.

Rub salmon with lemon juice and season with salt and pepper.

Place salmon in steamer basket and steam until pink inside, about 10 minutes.

Test for doneness by poking the thickest part with a knife. The fish should flake.

Transfer to a plate. Remove skin and chill until ready to serve.

Garnish salmon with lemons and fresh dill sprigs.

Serve with cucumber dill sauce.

Cucumber Dill Sauce

Combine all ingredients and chill.
Best made the day before.

Chicken & Artichokes

with Mushrooms

The rich sherry cream sauce makes this chicken dish a savory family favorite.

Serves 4

- 4 one half boneless chicken breasts, skinned
- 1½ sticks butter
- 2 lemons
- ¼ cup sherry or to taste
- 1 can artichoke hearts
- 1 cup mushrooms, sliced
- 1½ pint heavy cream, room temperature
- ½ cup Parmesan cheese

Preheat oven to 350 degrees F.

Pound chicken breasts between wax paper until thin.

In a skillet, sauté chicken in ½ stick butter until slightly brown on each side. Salt and pepper to taste. Remove and place in casserole.

In the same skillet, melt additional stick of butter and sauté mushrooms until tender. Remove and add to casserole with chicken. Add artichoke hearts.

Remove rind from lemons and sprinkle over chicken and vegetables.

Squeeze juice from 2 lemons and add to remaining butter in skillet, stirring over high heat.

Add sherry, stirring constantly.

Remove while butter is warm and stir in heavy cream.

Pour over chicken and dot with cheese. Bake for 30 minutes. Serve with rice or risotto.

Bavarian Beef
and Noodles

This is another recipe from Chef Jim Gregory's cookbook, published in 1974. Juniper berries and red currant jelly are the secret ingredients. This dish is best made the day before. Do not omit the croutons in the noodles!

Serves 8

½ lb. bacon
1 medium onion, diced
3 lb. beef stew meat, cut into 1 inch cubes
2 cloves garlic, chopped
½ cup flour
four friends: Maggi, Accent, Worcestershire sauce, Tabasco
½ cup tomato puree
1 small leek, washed and chopped
6 juniper berries or a small jigger of gin
2 tbsp. beef base
2 cans beer
1 lb. mushroom caps, washed
½ cup currant jelly
1 cup small pearl onions
3 tbsp. parsley, chopped

In a heavy stock pot, cook bacon until it is almost done. Drain off excess fat. Cut bacon into small pieces and add onion. Cook until the onion is transparent. Sear beef in bacon and onion until it is "gray" in color, not brown. Add garlic and sprinkle with flour. Stir until flour is absorbed. Add "four friends," tomato puree, leek, juniper berries, beef base, and beer.

Stir. Bring to boiling point, deglazing the bottom of the pan. Reduce heat and simmer, uncovered for 45–60 minutes or until beef is tender.

Add mushrooms, currant jelly, pearl onions, and parsley and cook for 15–20 minutes. Best made the day before. Serve with noodles.

Bavarian Noodles

8 oz. homemade type noodles
2 tbsp. butter
2 tbsp. oil
1 medium onion, sautéed in butter
¼ cup chopped parsley
1 cup seasoned croutons

Bavarian Noodles

Preheat oven to 350 degrees F.

Cook noodles in boiling salted water until tender. Drain and add butter, oil, sautéed onion, parsley, and croutons.

Toss together and place in a buttered casserole. Bake 15 minutes and serve hot with Bavarian Beef.

Chicken Curry

Fresh ginger and chutney are the key ingredients that make this chicken curry dish party fare. Be sure to make enough sauce as it is, indeed, the best part!

Serves 4

4 half chicken breasts
1 stick butter
1 large onion, diced
2 medium apples, diced
4 tbsp. fresh ginger, minced
3 tsp. curry powder (or to taste)
3 cups heavy cream, room temperature
8 oz. chutney sauce

Preheat oven to 350 degrees F.

Arrange chicken breasts in baking pan. Cover with 1 cup heavy cream. Bake 20 minutes.

Remove from oven. Place chicken in a casserole dish. Discard excess cream.

In a skillet, sauté butter and diced onion.

Add apples and minced ginger, cooking over moderately low heat.

Slowly stir in 2 cups heavy cream and cook until mixture is slightly thickened.

Remove from heat and whisk in curry powder and chutney.

Bake chicken and sauce in a casserole for 30 minutes.

Serve with rice and garnish with chopped parsley.

Lamb Stew

Although lamb is associated with spring, it is a treat during the fall and winter, too. Yeast dinner rolls are the perfect accompaniment to soak up the delicious gravy.

Serves 4

- 2 lb. boneless leg of lamb
- 3 tbsp. olive oil
- 2 yellow onions
- 2 tbsp. flour
- 3 cans beef broth
- 1 cup water
- 1 cup white wine
- 3 large carrots, peeled and cut into strips
- 3 stalks of celery, cut into strips
- 3 turnips, quartered
- 1 cup of peas, frozen

Cut lamb into large chunks. In a deep dish baking casserole, sauté lamb in olive oil. Add onions and continue to brown.

Coat with flour, stirring constantly.

Add beef broth, water and wine. Bring to a boil.

Reduce heat and simmer for 1½ hours or until lamb is tender.

Add carrots, celery, and turnips. Cook for 20 minutes.

Remove from heat. Refrigerate overnight.

Skim fat from top of stew.

Add 1 cup of frozen peas and cook over medium heat for 15 minutes until ready to serve.

Hearty Lasagna

This dish is a labor of love and well worth the time and effort to please family and friends.

Serves 8

2 tbsp. olive oil
1 cup chopped yellow onion
2 garlic cloves, minced
1 ½ lb. sweet Italian sausage, casings removed
1 28 oz. can crushed tomatoes
1 6 oz. can tomato paste
¼ cup fresh chopped parsley, divided
¼ cup fresh chopped oregano
¾ cup fresh basil leaves, chopped
salt and black pepper to taste
½ lb. lasagna noodles
16 oz. ricotta cheese
4 oz. creamy goat cheese, crumbled
1½ cup grated Parmesan cheese, divided
1 lb. fresh mozzarella cheese, thinly sliced
1 extra large egg, slightly beaten

Preheat oven to 400 degrees F.

In a large skillet heat olive oil. Add onion and cook until translucent, about 5 minutes. Add garlic and cook for 1 minute more. Add sausage and cook until it is no longer pink, breaking it up into small pieces as it cooks. Add tomatoes, tomato paste, 2 tbsp. parsley, basil, half the oregano, 1½ tsp. salt, and ½ tsp. pepper. Over medium low heat, simmer uncovered for 15–20 minutes, until thickened.

Fill a large bowl with the hottest possible tap water. Add the lasagna noodles and allow them to remain in the water for 20 minutes. Drain. In a separate bowl, combine ricotta, goat cheese, Parmesan, egg, remaining parsley and oregano, ½ tsp. salt, and ¼ tsp. pepper. Set aside.

Ladle on third of sauce into a 12 x 9 x 2 inch baking dish, spreading evenly over the bottom.

Add layers in the following order: half of the lasagna, half of the mozzarella, half of the ricotta mixture, and the second third of the sauce. Add the rest of the pasta, mozzarella, ricotta, and sauce. Sprinkle with ½ cup Parmesan cheese.

Bake 30 minutes or until sauce is bubbling.

To make ahead, refrigerate assembled unbaked lasagna. Bake 30–40 minutes until bubbly.

Pork Tenderloin

with Cherry Sauce

This recipe was in vogue decades ago and is still popular for dinner parties today.

Serves 4–6

1 1 lb. packaged pork tenderloin
olive oil
¼ cup fennel seed
10 oz. dried tart cherries
¾ bottle quality red wine
3 tbsp. butter

Preheat oven to 350 degrees F.

Prepare pork tenderloin at room temperature.

Brush with olive oil and fennel seed.

Grill over medium hot charcoal fire or bake in oven for 35 minutes.

Remove to heated platter and cover loosely with foil. Do not overcook.

Combine cherries and wine in a saucepan. Bring to a boil. Lower to simmer, uncovered until reduced by half.

Cut butter into small pieces. Over very low heat, swirl into sauce.

Serve sauce over tenderloin sliced on the diagonal.

Mustard Cream

Red Snapper

The sauce is the magic! It can accompany other fish, including salmon, and even chicken or pasta.

Serves 4

4 8 oz. red snapper fillets
8 oz. crème fraiche
2 tbsp. mayonnaise
3 tbsp. Dijon mustard
1 tbsp. whole grain mustard
1 tbsp. horseradish
1 tsp. fresh lemon juice
2 tbsp. minced shallots
2 tsp. drained capers
salt and pepper to taste

Preheat oven to 425 degrees F.

Place fish fillets skin side down in a stoneware baking dish. Season generously with salt and pepper.

In a small bowl, mix together crème fraiche, mayonnaise, 2 mustards, horseradish, lemon juice, shallots, capers, and 1 tsp. salt.

Spread sauce evenly over fish, covering completely.

Bake 10–15 minutes, depending on the thickness of the fish. The fish will flake easily at the thickest part when done.

Serve hot with extra sauce from the pan.

Chicken and Pasta

Casserole

This recipe fills the bill for a very hungry family and it lends itself to variations if you feel inventive.

Serves 10–12

1 lb. campanelle or rotini pasta
1 onion, diced
1 red pepper, julienne
1 zucchini, diced
½ tbsp. olive oil
½ tsp. dried Italian dressing
2 cups artichoke hearts, large, chopped
¼ cup black olives, sliced
2 cups tomatoes, diced
1 stick butter
½ cup flour
4 cups half & half cream
1 cup white wine
1 cup chicken broth
6 8 oz. boneless/skinless chicken breasts
2 cups mozzarella cheese, shredded
½ cup fresh bread crumbs
1 cup pesto sauce

Preheat oven to 350 degrees F.

Cook pasta al dente.

Sautee onion, pepper, and zucchini in skillet with olive oil and Italian seasoning. Add artichokes, black olives and tomatoes. Fold into the cooked pasta.

For the sauce, combine butter and flour. Cook roux until lightly brown. Stir in room temperature half & half cream. Add wine and broth. Cook until thickened.

Add sauce to pasta and vegetable mixture.

Bake chicken breasts in oven 18–20 minutes. Cut into pieces.

Place half of the pasta/vegetable mixture in a prepared dish.

Sprinkle with bread crumbs, cheese, and half the pesto sauce. Top with chicken.

Add remaining pasta/vegetable mixture. Top with pesto and cheese. Cover and bake for 1 hour until hot and bubbly.

Pot Roast

1950s Style

This is my grandmother's recipe that has not changed in decades. Add a generous splash of red wine to make this comfort food favorite even more perfect for a cold winter night's dinner.

Serves 4

- 1½ lb. boneless chuck steak, 2 inches thick
- 1 tsp. minced garlic
- ¼ cup flour
- ½ tsp. salt
- ¼ tsp. black pepper
- 2 tbsp. light olive oil
- 2 large onions sliced
- ½ cup celery, diced
- ½ cup carrots, sliced
- 1 lb. can tomatoes, chopped
- 1 cup beef broth
- ½ cup red wine (optional)
- 2 tsp. parsley chopped

Preheat oven to 300 degrees F.

Rub meat with garlic. Combine flour, salt and pepper. With a meat mallet, pound flour mixture into meat.

In a Dutch oven, heat oil over medium high temperature. Add meat and brown well on both sides.

Remove meat to a separate plate. Add onions, celery, and carrots to Dutch oven. Cook, about 5 minutes, stirring occasionally until golden.

Add tomatoes, beef broth, and red wine. Bring to a simmer.

Return meat to pot. Cover and bake 2–2½ hours until meat is fork tender.

Cool and chill overnight.

With a slotted spoon, remove fat from sauce in Dutch oven. Heat sauce and pot roast to boiling and cook 5 minutes. Simmer until ready to serve.

Stir in parsley.

Desserts

Chocolate Mousse

Grand Marnier Sauce for Fresh Fruit

Chocolate Chunk Cookies

Fruit Crumble

Warm Chocolate Lava Cake

Fresh Fruit Brûlée

Pumpkin Pie Bars

Lemon Raspberry Bread Pudding

Mocha Toffee Ice Cream Torte
with Hot Chocolate Sauce

Poached Pears

Chocolate Mousse

There is nothing more special than serving chocolate mousse at the end of a dinner party. It is elegant and easy and best made the day before. I particularly enjoy using heirloom porcelain lined silver cream soup bowls accompanied with Pirouette cookies served in a vintage silver cigarette box.

Serves 12

- 8 oz. semisweet chocolate
- 4 oz. unsweetened chocolate
- 1 cup sugar
- ⅔ cup water
- 6 egg yolks, beaten
- ¼ cup Amaretto or 2 tbsp. almond extract
- 1 quart heavy cream, whipped

Pulse chocolate in food processor until smooth.

Make simple syrup by combining sugar and water in a small sauce pan. Bring to a boil stirring constantly for 2 minutes.

Remove from stovetop. Pour simple syrup into chocolate while food processor is running. With a spatula, scrape down sides of mixture.

Add egg yolks and Amaretto. Blend again and cool.

Fold chocolate mixture into whipped cream.

Chill overnight.

Serve with whipped cream, shaved chocolate, pirouette cookies, and raspberries (optional).

Grand Marnier Sauce

for Fresh Fruit

Thank you, again, Chef Jim Gregory, for this family favorite recipe from the late 1960s. It is a keeper!

Serves 4

4 egg yolks, beaten
¾ cup sugar
1 tsp. lemon juice
1 dash salt
2 tbsp. flour
½ cup Grand Marnier
¼ cup frozen orange juice concentrate
½ pint heavy cream, whipped

In top of a double boiler, whisk together egg yolks, sugar, lemon juice, and salt.

Make a paste of flour, Grand Marnier, and juice concentrate. Add to mixture.

Cook over hot water, stirring constantly until thick. Cool.

Fold in whipped cream.

Serve with fresh seasonal fruit.

Chocolate Chunk
Cookies

For the chocolate lover, these decadent cookies fill the bill. The secret ingredient is sweetened condensed milk. If you are in a hurry or choose not to chill the dough, the baked cookies are still delicious and resemble thin brownies.

Makes 30

1 12 oz. bag semi-sweet chocolate chips
¾ stick butter, melted
1 cup flour
1 14 oz. can sweetened condensed milk
1 tsp. vanilla
2 cups semi-sweet chocolate chunks
4 tbsp. powdered sugar

Preheat oven to 325 degrees F.

Melt chocolate and butter in a sauce pan or microwave.

Combine flour, sweetened milk, and vanilla in a bowl. Add warm chocolate and mix thoroughly.

Fold in the chocolate chunks.

Refrigerate for 30 minutes.

Form one inch balls and place on a cookie sheet. Bake about 10 minutes. Cool on cookie rack.

Sprinkle with powdered sugar and serve.

Fruit Crumble

Crumbles have enhanced fruit for decades and their popularity does not seem to wane. Grandchildren can help mix the crumble ingredients. Little fingers are encouraged, creating happy cooking experiences!

Serves 8

Basic Topping

1 cup flour
¾ cup quick cooking oats
1 cup brown sugar
½ cup white sugar
¼ tsp. salt
12 tbsp. unsalted butter, room temperature

Combine flour, oats, sugars and salt in a large bowl. Knead mixture and butter with fingers or mix on low speed until consistency is crumbly. Set aside.

Fruit Variations

Apples and Cranberries

2 12 oz. packages of cranberries
4 assorted apples, cored and cut into ½ inch cubes
1 cup granulated sugar
3 tbsp. apple juice or cider
1 tsp. cinnamon

Preheat oven to 375 degrees F. Butter a 12 x 9 x 2 inch baking dish. Combine cranberries, apples, sugar, juice, and cinnamon in a large pot. Boil until cranberries are tender and apples are soft, about 10 minutes. Transfer filling to baking dish. Top with crumble mixture and bake for 45 minutes. Serve warm.

Strawberries, Blueberries, Raspberries, and Peaches

3 peaches, chopped
1 cup blueberries
1 cup strawberries, chopped
1 cup raspberries
¼ cup granulated sugar
¼ cup flour
1 tbsp. fresh lemon juice

Preheat oven to 375 degrees F. Combine fruit, sugar, flour, and lemon juice in a large bowl. Toss to mix well. Pour mixture into a 12 x 9 x 2 inch baking dish. Top with crumble mixture and bake for 1 hour or until bubbly and the top is golden brown. Serve warm.

Warm Chocolate

Lava Cake

This decadent dessert always intrigues guests. The rich chocolate sauce oozing out of the cake is a pleasant surprise. Ovens vary and this recipe is time and temperature sensitive. It may require a trial run. Coating the ramekins with shortening instead of butter is the secret for turning the cakes out onto plates.

Serves 4

1 tbsp. vegetable shortening for molds
cocoa powder for molds
½ cup unsalted butter
4 oz. bittersweet chocolate
2 large eggs
2 large egg yolks
¼ cup sugar
2 tsp. all-purpose flour
½ tsp. vanilla extract
pinch of salt

Preheat oven to 450 degrees F.

Smear with vegetable shortening four 3 inch ramekin molds and dust the inside lightly with cocoa powder, tilting to coat. Tap out excess and set aside. Chill briefly.

Heat butter and chocolate in a double boiler until chocolate is melted. Cool slightly.

In a bowl with an electric mixer, whisk together eggs, egg yolks, and sugar until light and thick.

Slowly add chocolate mixture to eggs and sugar. Stir in flour, vanilla extract, and salt.

Divide batter among prepared ramekins. Place on a baking sheet and into the oven. Bake 7–10 minutes until sides are set and the center is soft.

Remove from oven. Let stand 5 minutes.

Invert each mold onto a plate. Gently tap the tops of molds and carefully lift to remove. Sprinkle with confectioners' sugar and serve immediately.

Serve with small scoops of pistachio ice cream.

Fresh Fruit Brûlée

Move over "créme" brûlée for a colorful and delicious change! The only fussy part of this recipe is that it requires last minute attention, but your family or guests will appreciate your effort.

Serves 6–8

4 cups fresh fruit, cut up
½ cup granulated sugar
½ cup Grand Marnier
1 pint of heavy or extra heavy whipping cream
1 cup brown sugar

Combine fresh fruit and sugar in a large bowl. Douse with Grand Marnier.

Transfer to a baking dish. Cover with whipped cream and brown sugar.

Chill in freezer up to an hour.

Place under broiler and let caramelize before serving.

Remove from oven and serve immediately.

Pumpkin Pie Bars

These seasonal dessert bars are perfect for a tail gate picnic or a holiday party. Serve warm with ice cream for a special treat.

Makes 2 dozen

1½ cups of flour
½ cup firmly packed brown sugar
¾ cup granulated sugar, divided
¾ cup butter
3 eggs
1 8 oz. package cream cheese
1 15 oz. can of pumpkin
1 tsp. pumpkin pie spice
1 cup quick cooking oats
½ cup chopped pecans

Preheat oven to 350 degrees F.

Line a 12 x 9 x 2 inch baking pan with foil with the end of foil extending over the sides. Grease foil with butter.

Mix together flour, brown sugar, ¼ cup sugar. Cut in butter with pastry blender or fingers until mixture resembles coarse crumbs.

Stir in oats and pecans. Reserve 1 cup of mixture. Press remaining mixture onto bottom of pan. Bake for 15 minutes.

Beat cream cheese, remaining ½ cup sugar, eggs, pumpkin, and pumpkin pie spice with electric mixer on medium until well blended.

Pour over crust and sprinkle with reserved crumb mixture. Bake 25 minutes.

Cut into bars when cool. Store in refrigerator.

Lemon Raspberry
Bread Pudding

Bread pudding comes in many varieties and this is a refreshing change from traditional recipes.

Serves 8

2 pints raspberries
1 loaf Italian bread, crust on, cut into ¾ inch pieces (about 4½ cups)
2 cups milk
2½ cups heavy whipping cream
¾ cup granulated sugar
¼ tsp. salt
zest of 3 lemons
3 large eggs
3 large egg yolks
¼ tsp. cinnamon
1½ tbsp. sugar

Preheat oven to 350 degrees F.

Spread 1 pint of raspberries evenly on the bottom of a 12 x 9 x 2 inch baking pan. Place bread pieces on top of fruit.

Heat milk, cream, sugar, salt, and lemon zest in a saucepan over medium heat, stirring frequently about 5 minutes until liquid is very hot and sugar has dissolved.

Whisk together eggs and egg yolks in a large bowl.

Whisk hot cream mixture into the eggs, a little at a time.

Pour custard into the pan over raspberries and bread pieces.

Using a spatula, press the bread pieces into the custard, coating them well. Bake for 40 minutes.

While pudding is baking, combine cinnamon and sugar in a small bowl.

Sprinkle cinnamon sugar over pudding and continue baking 10 minutes more until tips of bread pieces are golden brown and a small knife inserted in the middle is coated with thickened custard.

Let cool 15 minutes. Serve warm with the other pint of raspberries.

Mocha Toffee

Ice Cream Torte with Hot Chocolate Sauce

Do not serve this dessert after a heavy meal! Provide guests their own containers of hot chocolate sauce. It is a fun idea that is always well received.

Serves 12

1 box Famous Chocolate Wafer cookies
8 tbsp. butter, melted
4 pints mocha chocolate chip ice cream
¼ cup Kahlua
1½ cups crushed toffee bars (8)

Crush chocolate cookie wafers in a plastic bag with a rolling pin. Add to melted butter and spread onto the bottom and sides of a 9 inch buttered spring-form pan. Bake in a 350 degree oven for 5 minutes. Cool.

Place a sheet of aluminum foil under the spring-form pan and wrap around the sides of the pan. Place 2 pints of softened ice cream in bottom of spring-form pan. Sprinkle with ¾ cups of crushed toffee and 3 tbsp. of Kahlua. Repeat with remaining 2 pints of ice cream, toffee and Kahlua. Cover with foil and place in freezer until firm and ready to serve. Slice and serve with hot chocolate sauce.

Makes 3 Cups

Hot Chocolate Sauce

8 oz. milk chocolate (2 bars German chocolate)
½ cup water
2 tsp. instant coffee powder
2 tbsp. cornstarch
¼ tsp. salt
1 cup heavy cream
½ cup sherry

Hot Chocolate Sauce

Melt chocolate and water together in sauce pan over low heat until chocolate melts. Combine remaining ingredients in bowl. Add to chocolate and bring to a boil. Cook, stirring constantly, for 5 minutes or more until mixture thickens. Cool. Reheat and serve warm with Mocha Toffee Ice Cream Torte.

Poached Pears

These are a healthy fall or warm winter treat that is always a hit. Serve in pretty bowls on treasured heirloom plates.

Serves 6

6 medium pears, unskinned (1 per person)
3 cups dark brown sugar
1 bottle good red cooking wine
6 cinnamon sticks
6 whole cloves
4 oranges and 4 lemons, sliced
1 pint heavy cream, whipped (garnish)
toasted almonds (garnish)

Preheat oven to 375 degrees F.

Halve pears and place in shallow baking pan skin side up.

Combine sugar and wine. Pour over pears.

Scatter cinnamon sticks, cloves and fruit slices.

Bake for 45 minutes. Remove cinnamon, cloves, and fruit.

Transfer pears to a serving dish or individual plates.

Serve warm with whipped cream and toasted almonds.

Some of my earliest days of having fun were in the attic of my childhood home making craft projects from little plastic charms, paper flowers, and brightly colored sequins. My mother had saved this Pogue's department store box full of vintage trinkets that bring back fond memories.

Entertaining

4

Today, my idea of having fun is entertaining. It is the opportunity to bring together good friends and family, to use pretty things when preparing and presenting delicious food, and to create warm feelings that result in special memories.

The real fun starts with the invitation and creating anticipation for guests before the party or event occurs. Designing and making invitations that require extra postage or that can be hand delivered is old fashioned and quite appreciated in today's world.

Much like playing dolls, it is fun to set our dining room table with beloved silver butter plates or with casual acrylic chargers and funky folded paper napkins. Better yet, set multiple tables with different themes using separate china and linens. The more moving pieces to assemble and style, the more fun!

Arrange flowers in biscuit barrels, porcelain tureens or brass wall pockets. For place cards, use the slots of antique children's banks or candy that suggests a spouse's name like Anne's "Lifesaver" or Tom's "Tootsie Roll." Such thoughtful details are elements of gracious hospitality that evoke surprises and smiles.

What fun it is to put long, skinny breadsticks into individual silver bud vases or to serve salads in colorful Chinese carry out containers. Cold soup in a plastic shot glass topped with a crudité toothpick kabob works wonders for a picnic. Another twist is to use a collection of coffee creamers, full of hot chocolate sauce, giving each guest his/her own creamer to pour over an already decadent piece of Mocha Toffee Ice Cream Torte.

Having fun is mixing and matching ordinary items with treasured heirlooms and using them for different purposes. Included in this section are re-created samples of some fun invitations and announcements we have sent over the years, quirky ideas for food presentation, and a few thank you responses, some of which were made from the original party invitations of good pals. Having fun is an attitude. May we all continue to have fun appreciating and respecting tradition in creative ways and pass it along.

...thoughtful details are elements of gracious hospitality that evoke surprises and smiles.

LISA
The next best thing to baking cookies....
shopping at Crayons to Computers!
CRAYONS
Featuring
The Built-In Sharpener
64
64
CRAYONS
The Lone Ranger

Having Fun

CLUB
DINNER
MEETING
CRAYONS
mary ann
CRAYONS
16
gary
CRAYONS
24

Party Planning

I once hosted a dinner for a group at our Crayons to Computers' warehouse. The invitation was a spiral bound notebook complete with information about the evening, including directions. What fun it was to carry out the crayon theme on place cards, chargers, and in the selection of china, glassware, and table linens. Centerpieces were stacked boxes of crayons interspersed with school supplies.

Chinese carry out containers are fun to use as invitations for casual meals at home. Fill another clear container with confetti and noise makers for the dinner invitation to celebrate a special occasion. Extra postage is required in both cases! Better yet, consider hand delivering them to your guests' mailbox or front door.

Invitations & Announcements

Clockwise: A Western themed party invitation can start with store bought graphics, but adding a bandana in a craft bag adds more anticipation to the event. • A child's birthday party invitation idea using toy dinosaurs: "A dino party plea ... Cooper-osauraus is turning three! • Include in a festive plastic bag all the fixings for "s'more" reasons to toast a couple's engagement. • A moving announcement can be made, literally, from packing materials.

A spatula attached to an invitation is a practical and fun holiday gift.

Our Castle parties were always a big hit, especially when the sliders were served in see-through carry out containers with fluorescent paper and up lights.

Dessert can be equally fun when cupcakes are perched on top of plastic skirted "tables" only to hide an ice cream smoothie underneath! The container triples as a fingerbowl at the end of the meal.

More Fun Ideas

Clockwise: Additional 3D invitations include those that use washcloths for a wedding shower or candy for an engagement announcement, "Here's the Scoop!" • A popsicle made from a Styrofoam noodle is the fun item on this invitation for a pool party. • A plastic mint julep cup doubles as an invitation for a Derby party. A vintage 45 record is used for a Rock n' Roll event. What little princess wouldn't enjoy having her own mirror, bow, and toe separators on a party invite?! • A graduation party invitation includes a doily placemat and faux diploma.

Small size lunch boxes make great invitations for full size box lunch picnics!

Thank You

It was our good fortune to be with you!
THANK YOU
sally & rick
Thank You!! For MOUNDS of Fun!
Try your luck...
and we DID!
with a big SCORE!
THANK YOU!!!
THANK YOU!
The Cat in the Hat has nothing on you. So come in a hat Oh Please Do Do Do!

What fun we have had collecting and entertaining together over the years!

My first "thank you" goes to my wonderful husband, Lee, and my longtime friend, Ann Reed, who both encouraged me to write this book.

I want to thank Marcy and Sarah Hawley and Alyson Rua at Orange Frazer Press who have helped make this project a reality.

I am so grateful to the amazing team of people who created the photographs for this book. Photographer Ryan Kurtz, stylist Jess Cundiff, and food stylist, Jeffrey Martin, are all extremely talented and dedicated. With the utmost attention to detail, they created incredibly beautiful images much like the stunning Flemish still life paintings of the 17th century. I never knew that our collections could look so inviting and our food so tempting.

Helping in the kitchen were Jeff's assistants, my longtime friend and caterer, Beth O'Leary, and her co-worker Christina Sofranec, whom I have known for decades. Peggy Neal filled in one day to keep operations running smoothly. Ryan and Jess also had assistants and I want to thank Ian Galloway, Natalie Jenkins, Ellen Stone, and Steve Ross who helped with equipment, props, and lighting. Their efforts were like a minuet, everyone stepping in the right direction at the right time to be as efficient and productive as possible. The sets they created were magical and remarkably full of energy and fun.

I will always be thankful to Mary March for a wonderful experience working with her. Our years together were so memorable.

Behind the scenes were friends who lent me fabrics and the empty picture frame: thank you Anthony Zalants of Hanover House and Mary Ran of Ran Gallery. Maurice Oshry's beautiful leather books and Dick Bere's antique fruit jars and country kitchen tools added great touches to some of the pictures.

Thank you Dawson Bullock and Angie Geier of Dawson Designs and Kristin Folzenlogen of Poeme for helping me re-create former invitations and announcements. Your graphic design talents are awesome!

I was inspired years ago by local chef, Jim Gregory, and national divas Martha Stewart, Sheila Chavetz, and Perry Wolfman, all of whom I had the pleasure of meeting.

Family members and friends have also been inspirations to me and that list, unfortunately, is too long to include. You know who you are and I am forever appreciative of our friendship.

Thank you again to my best friend, Lee, who is my North Star and my strongest critic and supporter ever. What fun we have had collecting and entertaining together over the years!

Recipe Index

Asian Slaw, 134
Baby Beets topped with Boursin Cheese, 80
Bavarian Beef and Noodles, 170
Black Olive Curry Canapés, 82
Butternut Squash and Ginger Soup, 108
Chicken and Pasta Casserole, 182
Chicken Curry, 172
Chicken & Artichokes with Mushrooms, 168
Chilled Pasta Salad with Shrimp, 132
Chocolate Chunk Cookies, 192
Chocolate Mousse, 188
Cider Stewed Tomatoes, 152
Cold Steamed Salmon, 166
Cold Tomato Soup, 102
Colorado Salad, 130
Creamed Spinach, 144
Curried Cream Cheese Consommé, 100
French Green Beans, 158
French Onion Soup, 104
Fresh Fruit Brûlée, 198
Fruit Crumble, 194
Garden Green Soup, 110
Gazpacho, 116
Grand Marnier Sauce for Fresh Fruit, 190
Hearty Lasagna, 176
Iced Borscht, 112
Kentucky Spoon Bread, 146
Lamb Stew, 174
Lemon Raspberry Bread Pudding, 202
Maple Ginger Roasted Vegetables, 150
Mini Cocktail Quiches, 86
Minted Pea Soup, 118
Mocha Toffee Ice Cream Torte
with Hot Chocolate Sauce, 204
Mustard Cream Red Snapper, 180
Mustard Tarragon Chicken Salad, 128
Netherland Salad, 126
Orzo Salad with Tomatoes, Feta, and Basil, 122
Oyster Crackers with Seasoning, 90
Parmesan Puffs, 94
Parmesan Tuilles, 78
Poached Pears, 206
Popovers, 154
Pork Tenderloin with Cherry Sauce, 178
Pot Roast 1950s Style, 184
Pumpkin Pie Bars, 200
Radicchio Cups with Bleu Cheese, 84
Ratatouille, 148
Roasted Cauliflower and Arugula Salad, 124
Seafood Cocktail Spread, 88
Simply Enhanced Soups, 106
Spiced Iced Tea, 160
Spicy Tortilla Wraps, 92
Summer Salad, 140
Sweet Potato Mash, 156
Tomato Aspic, 138
Vichysoisse, 114
Warm Chocolate Lava Cake, 196
Watercress and Feta Salad
with Curried Yogurt Dressing, 136
Watercress Sandwiches, 96
Yeast Dinner Rolls, 162